W9-CHG-157

A Little Seashore Book
by Bill Martin, Jr.
with John Archambault

with watercolors by Ted Rand

cassette recording
narrated by Bill Martin, Jr.
and John Archambault
with music by guitarist Al Caiola

Library of Congress Catalog Card No. 85-81423
ISBN: 0-8347-2965-2

**Bill
Martin's**

· LITTLE ·
SEASHORE
· BOOKS ·

The
Silent
Wetlands
Hold Back
the Sea

*A Read-Along
Series*

1

The sea rises...
the sea subsides...
the coming and going
 of high and low tides...
 lashing...
 splashing...
 against the shore...
sea and land
in an endless war...

2

...an endless war...
The waves...gray sea wolves...
    attack the prey...
        loosening...
        washing the shore away...
The silent land...
    stands...
        night and day...
        defending...
    holding the gnawing sea
    at bay...

3

The land stands...
    silently slowing
    the onslaught of the sea...
building up sand...
building up stretches of sand...
ridges of sand
becoming sandbars...
becoming barriers...

4

sand barriers...
trapping the sea's retreating tides...
trapping the seawater...
    in little pools...
trapping millions of seaplants
    and small sea creatures...
washed in by the tide...
caught in the pools...
    along the shore...

5

The pools of seawater…
    pools of sealife…
caught in shallow bowls of sand…
cradled along the shore…
are warmed by the sun…
nurturing…
nourishing
the growth of cord grass…
    nature's anomaly…
land's link with the sea…

6

Rough...tough...coarse...
    cord grass...
a plant from the land...
    not from the sea...
growing...thriving...
    in salt-sea pools...
spreading quickly...wildly
    in the sea-washed mud...
trapping sand
    as sand traps the sea...

7

Rough...tough...coarse...
    cord grass
is a quiet fortress
    built in the sand...
slowing the onslaught
    of the constant sea...
holding fast
    against incoming tides...
trapping more sealife
    as the tide subsides...

8

Tiny pools...along the shore...
holding an invisible world...
of living and dying...
new cord grass thriving...
old stalks dying...
decaying...
dissolving...
changing the pool
into a salty broth...
a rich soup
for hungry creatures...

9

The pools become chaos
at times of high tide...
churning commotion...
an invasion of waves...
tons of water
        swirling with sand...
        dumped on the cord grass...
        flooding the pools...

10

Millions of sea creatures
ride in with high tide...
ride over the sandbars...
ride over the barriers...
    carried ashore
    by the surging tide...
Clams...oysters...
mussels...shrimp...
fish of all sizes...
fish of all kinds...
    a bounty of sealife
    caught in the pools
    as the tide subsides...

11

As the tide subsides...
rolling back to the sea...
    over the sandbars...
    over the barriers...
the water is combed by cord grass...
    land's link with the sea...
rough...tough...
coarse...cord grass...
that filters the mud
and the sand from the water...
    enlarging the mudflats
    where cord grass can grow...

12

At low tide...
the beaches...the barriers...
the enlarging wetlands...
become feeding grounds
    for fish and for fowl...
Birds sweep in
    to eat the sea creatures
    left by the tide...
    exposed in the mud...
    an easy feast
    for hungry shore birds
    and migrating sea birds...
    stopping to feed...

13

Raccoons come too...
    hunting crabs and mussels...
    searching the muck
    for a tasty meal...
A host of other hungry hunters
crowd the beach...
crowd each other...
foraging the pools...
    the cord grass...
    the wetlands...
    for seafood delights...
    until the next high tide...
    when the sea returns...

14

The sea rises...
the sea subsides...
twice-daily sweeps
of high and low tides...
leaving a lacework
    of mudflats and sand...
    anchored by cord grass
    that links sea and land...
The wetlands...
a natural pantry
on the ocean shore...
    where sea and land
    wage endless war...